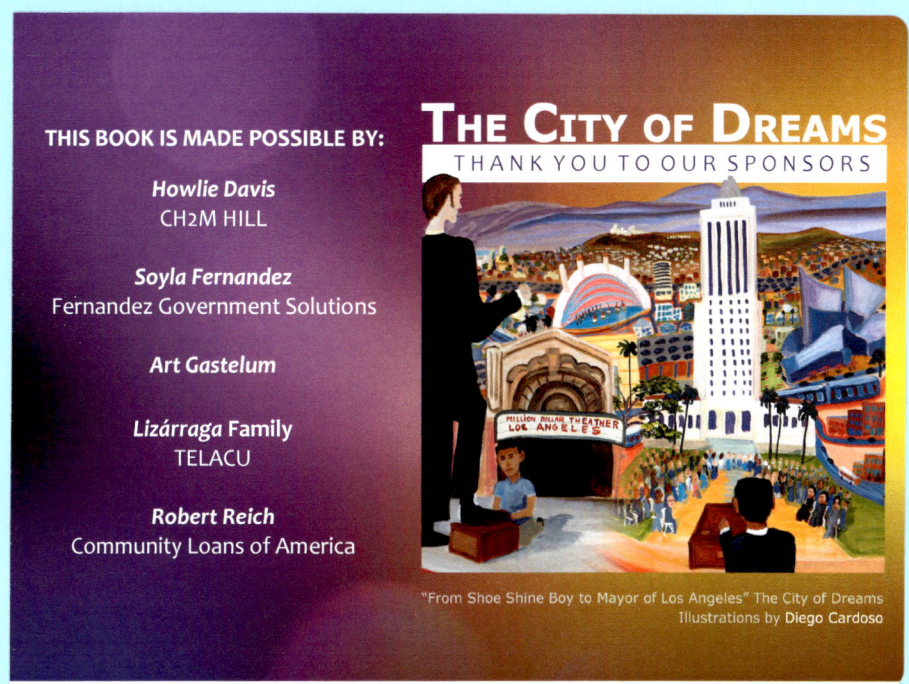

THIS BOOK IS MADE POSSIBLE BY:

Howlie Davis
CH2M HILL

Soyla Fernandez
Fernandez Government Solutions

Art Gastelum

Lizárraga Family
TELACU

Robert Reich
Community Loans of America

THE CITY OF DREAMS
THANK YOU TO OUR SPONSORS

"From Shoe Shine Boy to Mayor of Los Angeles" The City of Dreams
Illustrations by **Diego Cardoso**

Shine, Shine, Shine Bright

The Antonio Villaraigosa Story

Story by Josefina Lopez
Illustrations by Diego Cardoso

LA Plaza de Cultura y Artes • Los Angeles • California • 90012

Copyright © 2012 LA Plaza de Cultura y Artes

Illustrations Copyright © 2012 Diego Cardoso

Shine, Shine, Shine Bright

The Antonio Villaraigosa Story

Published by LA Plaza de Cultura y Artes • www.lapca.org

All rights reserved. No part of this publication may be reproduced, stored in a retrieval system, or transmitted in any form or by any means, electronic, mechanical, photocopying, recording, or otherwise without permission of the publisher. For information regarding permission, write to LA Plaza de Cultura y Artes, 501 North Main Street, Los Angeles, CA 90012 or info@lapca.org

ISBN 978-0-615-68109-2

10 9 8 7 6 5 4 3 2 1

Printed in the United States of America

This work is inspired by true events

Story by Josefina Lopez

Illustrations by Diego Cardoso

Los Angeles Latino Mayors historical recount prepared by
the Director of Education & Programs for LA Plaza de Cultura y Artes, Cindi Dale

To every child who dares to dream ...

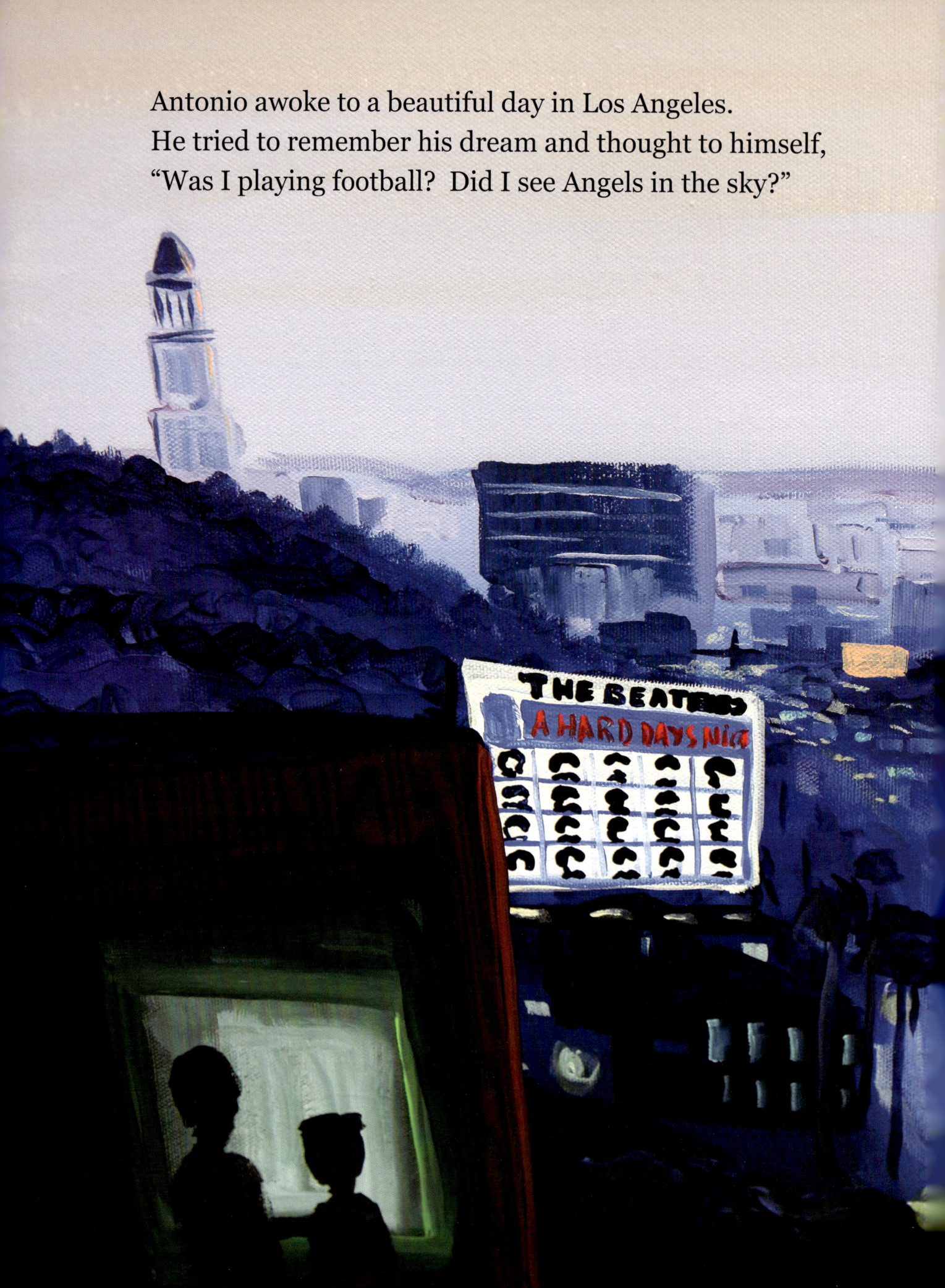

Antonio awoke to a beautiful day in Los Angeles. He tried to remember his dream and thought to himself, "Was I playing football? Did I see Angels in the sky?"

He heard his mother sigh, "Ay mijo, you are now the man of the house and together with your sisters we will all work to keep our family unified and strong!"

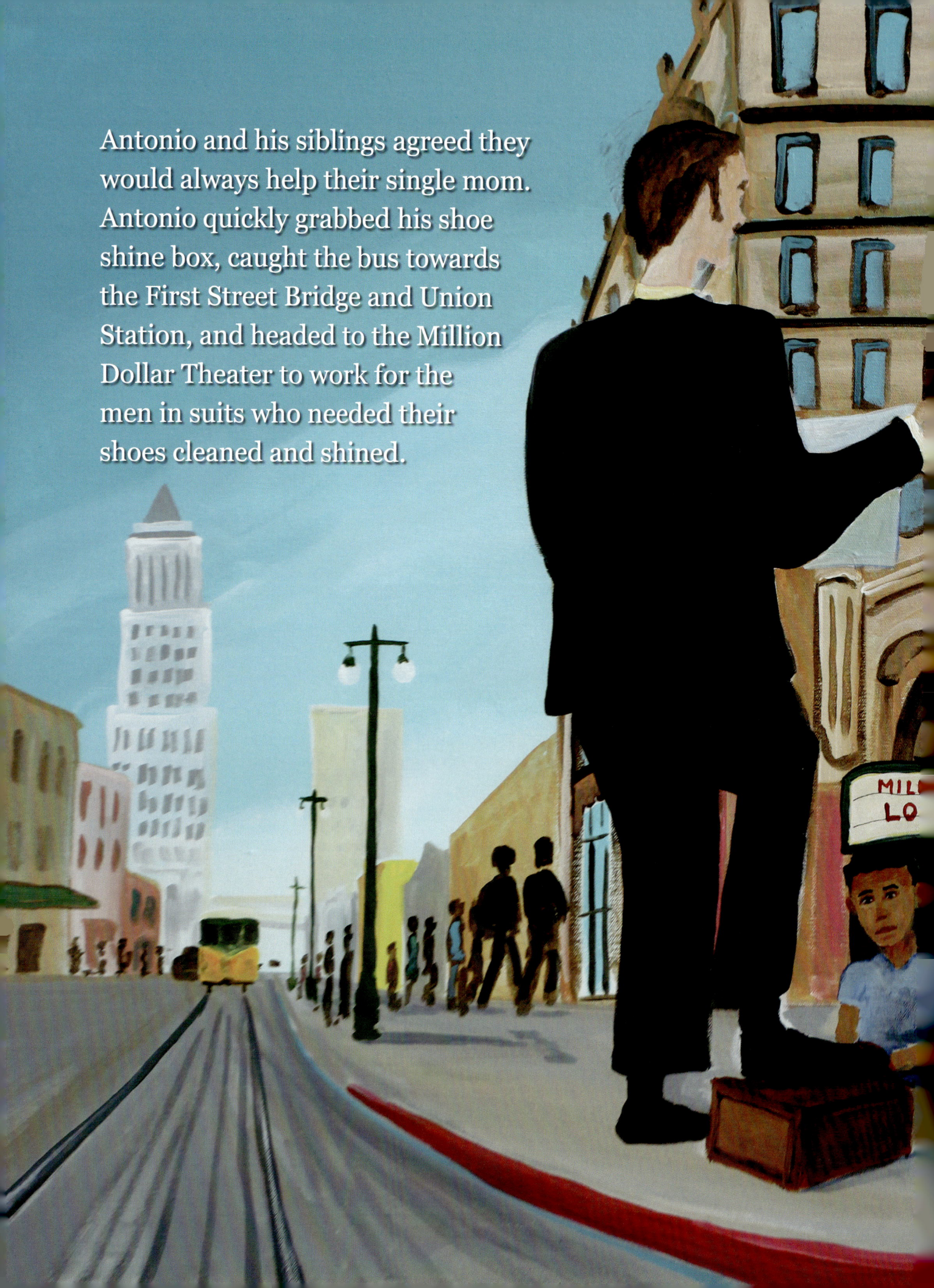

Antonio and his siblings agreed they would always help their single mom. Antonio quickly grabbed his shoe shine box, caught the bus towards the First Street Bridge and Union Station, and headed to the Million Dollar Theater to work for the men in suits who needed their shoes cleaned and shined.

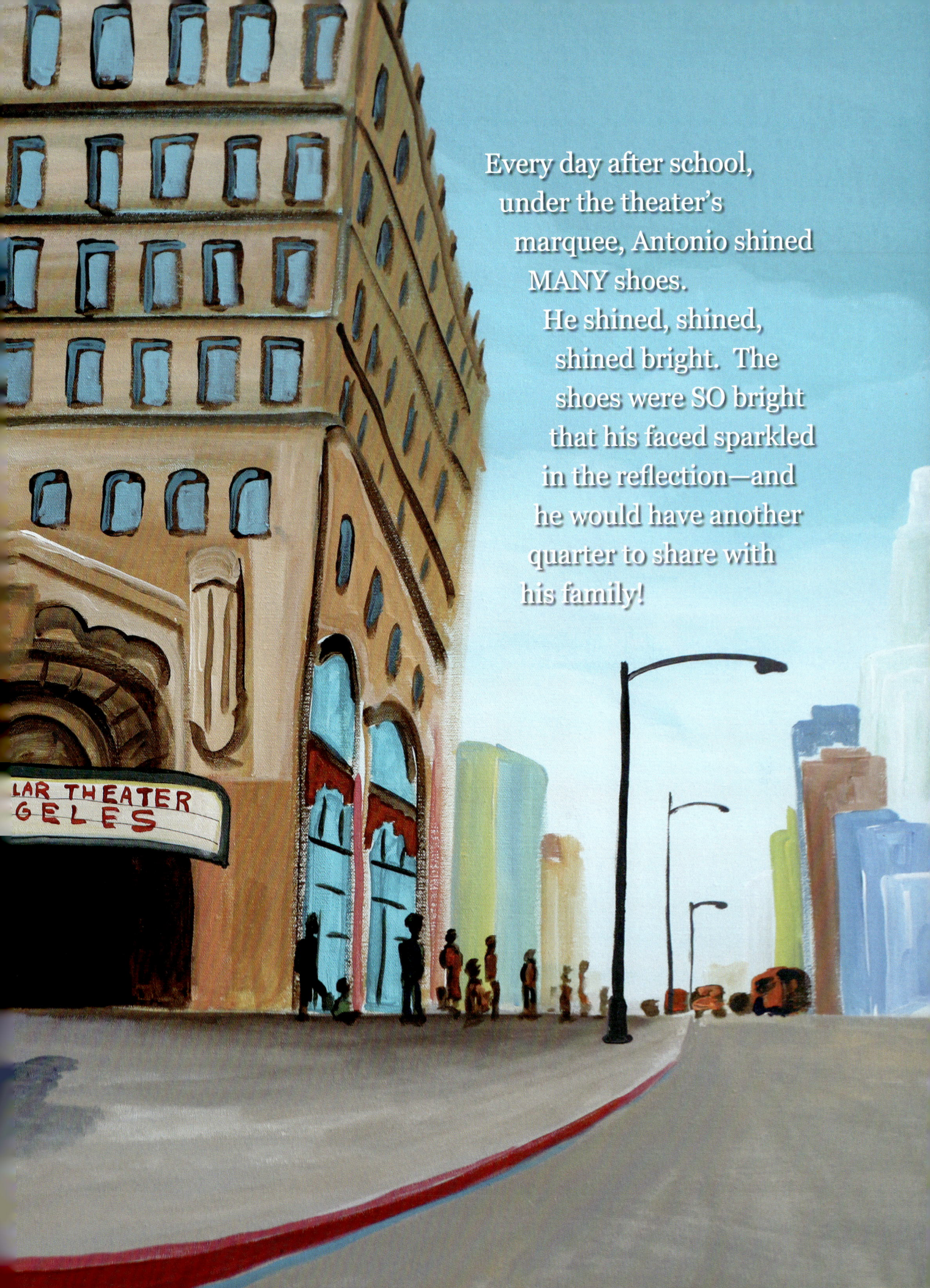

Every day after school, under the theater's marquee, Antonio shined MANY shoes. He shined, shined, shined bright. The shoes were SO bright that his faced sparkled in the reflection—and he would have another quarter to share with his family!

One day while shining shoes at Union Station, Antonio looked up at a man in his suit and tie reading a newspaper. He saw the picture of three Mexican-American men who long ago were Mayors of the City of Los Angeles: Antonio Franco Coronel, Manuel Requena and Cristobal Aguilar.

Wow, Antonio thought to himself—maybe one day I could be Mayor of Los Angeles!

The thought made him feel strong and positive.

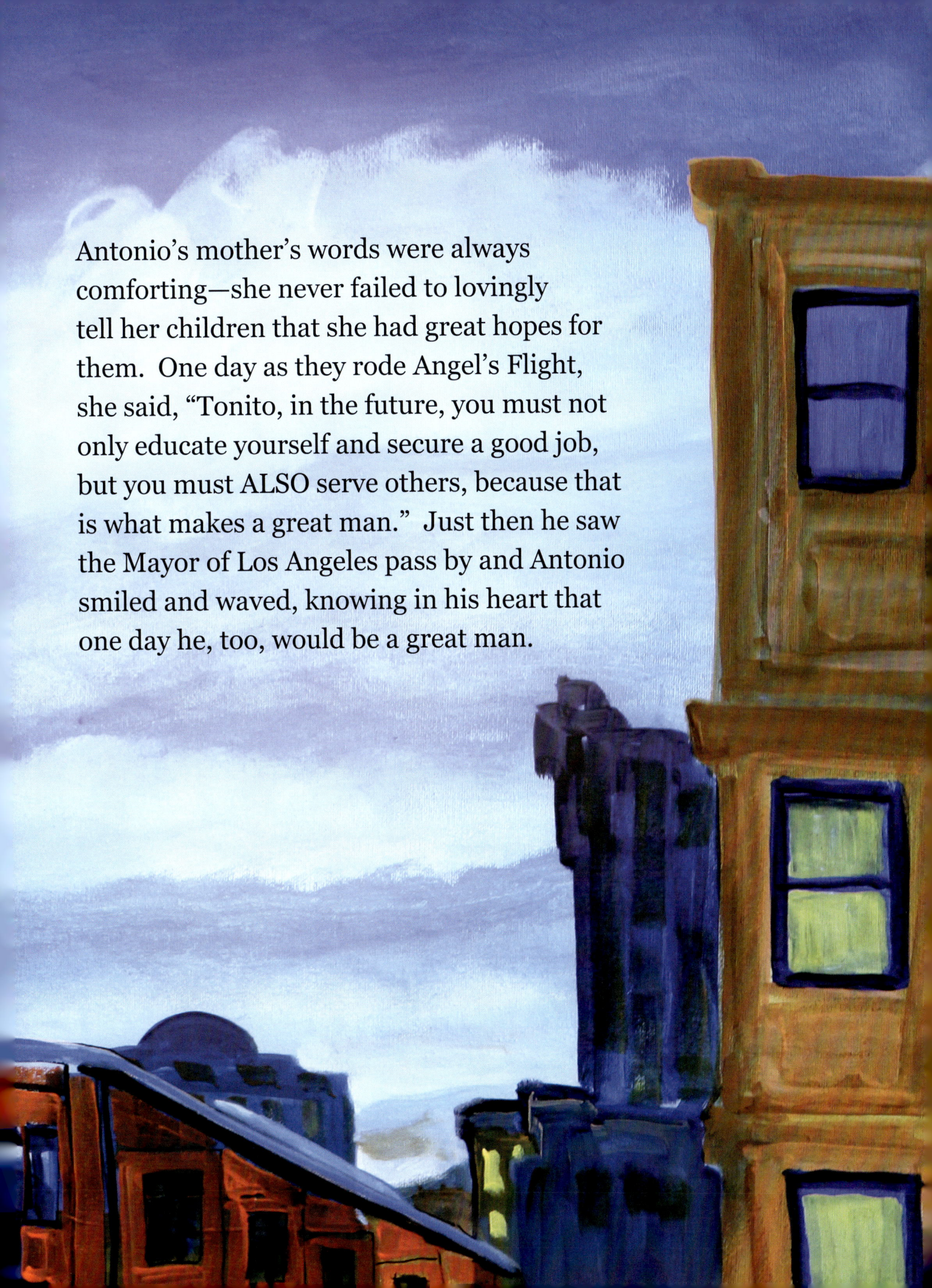

Antonio's mother's words were always comforting—she never failed to lovingly tell her children that she had great hopes for them. One day as they rode Angel's Flight, she said, "Tonito, in the future, you must not only educate yourself and secure a good job, but you must ALSO serve others, because that is what makes a great man." Just then he saw the Mayor of Los Angeles pass by and Antonio smiled and waved, knowing in his heart that one day he, too, would be a great man.

Studying was challenging for Antonio, because so many of his friends didn't care about learning—and they also believed that big dreams never came true for Latinos. Slowly Antonio began to believe it, too.

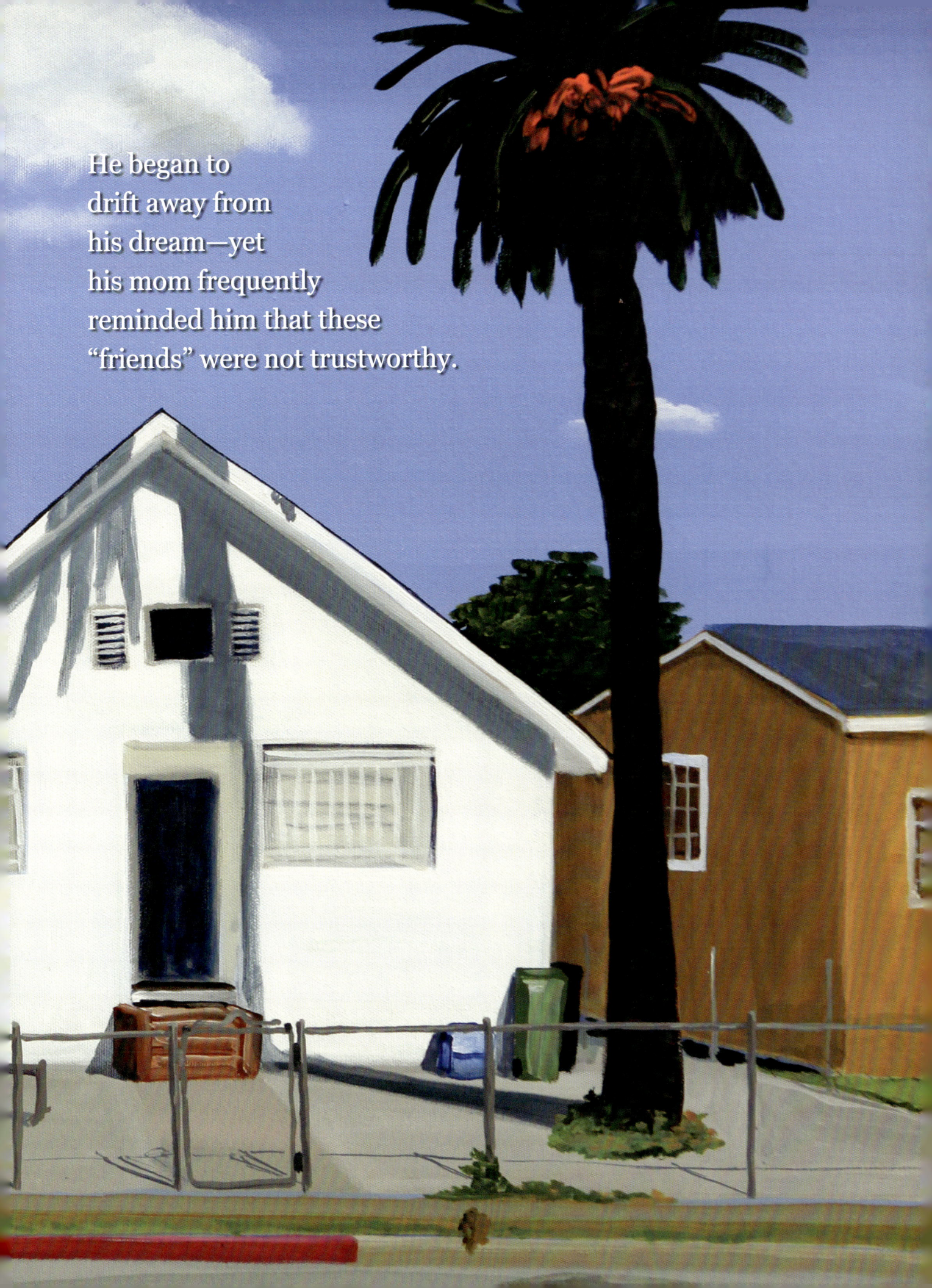

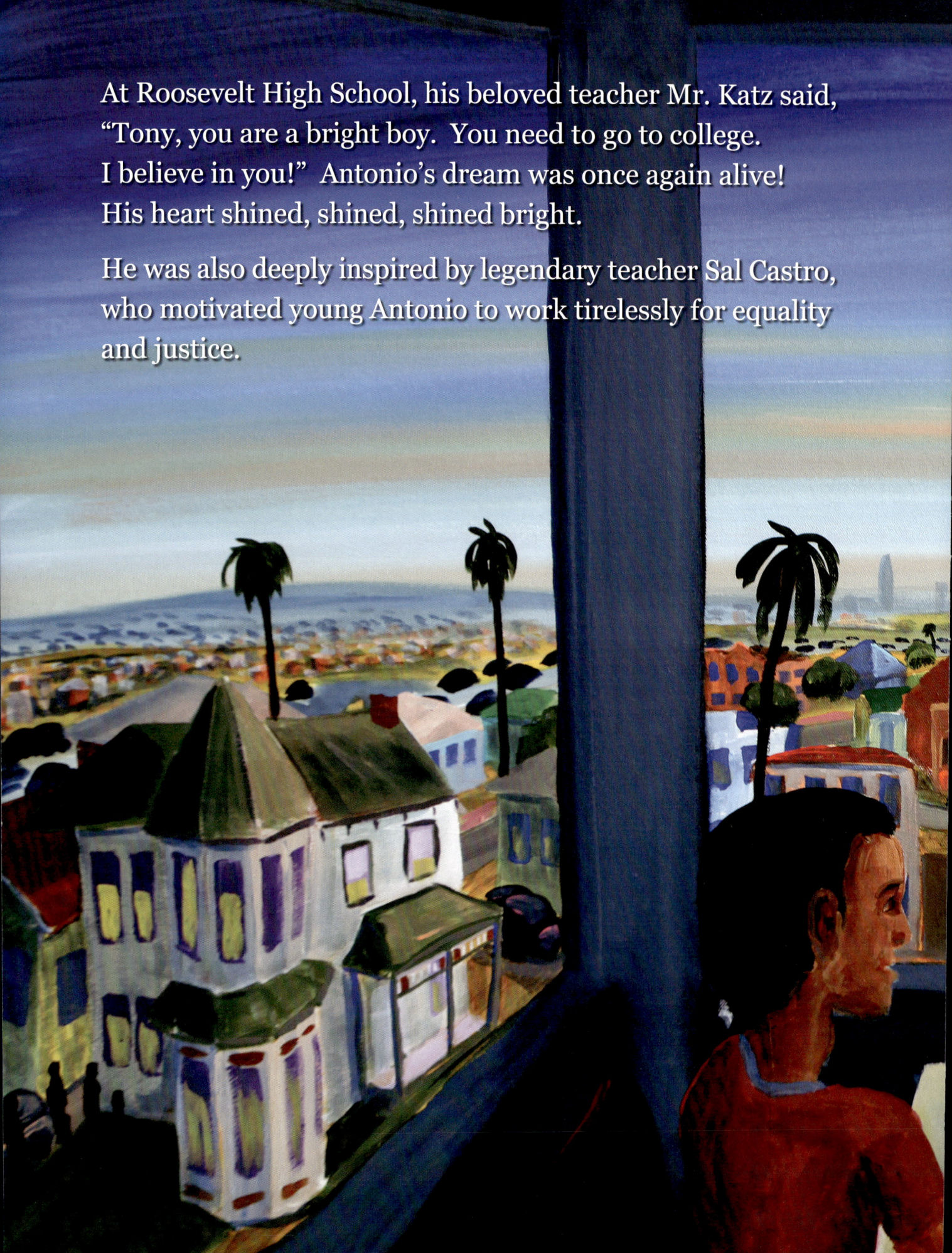

At Roosevelt High School, his beloved teacher Mr. Katz said, "Tony, you are a bright boy. You need to go to college. I believe in you!" Antonio's dream was once again alive! His heart shined, shined, shined bright.

He was also deeply inspired by legendary teacher Sal Castro, who motivated young Antonio to work tirelessly for equality and justice.

Antonio pondered the words of his mother and teachers, and was determined to graduate from college then return to work in the community he loved. He decided to attend UCLA!

Antonio also attended law school and worked for the devoted, hardworking men and women who are the backbone of our City.

He believed in the American Dream, he took pride in his children, and he became a gifted communicator and a respected community leader.

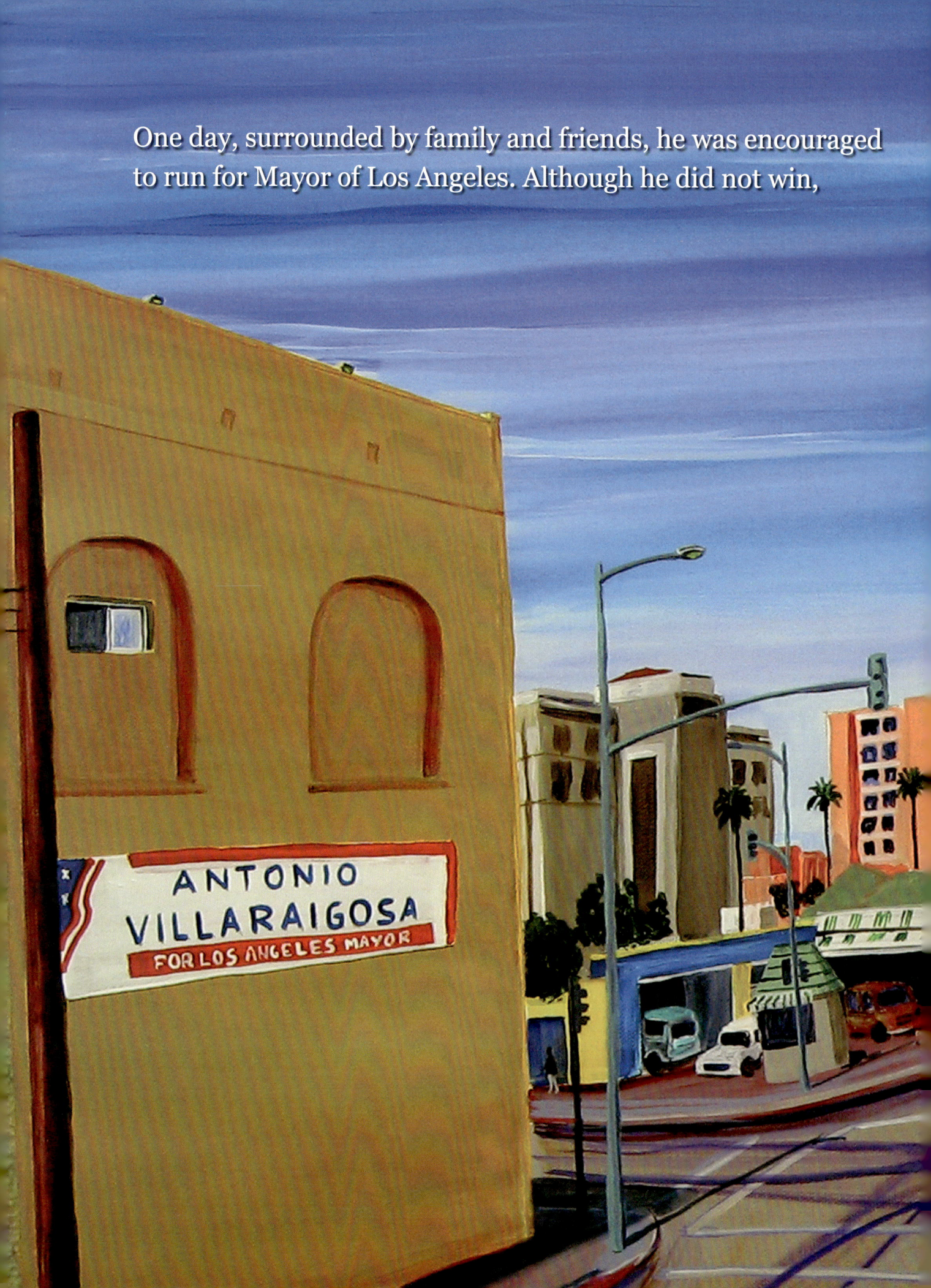

One day, surrounded by family and friends, he was encouraged to run for Mayor of Los Angeles. Although he did not win,

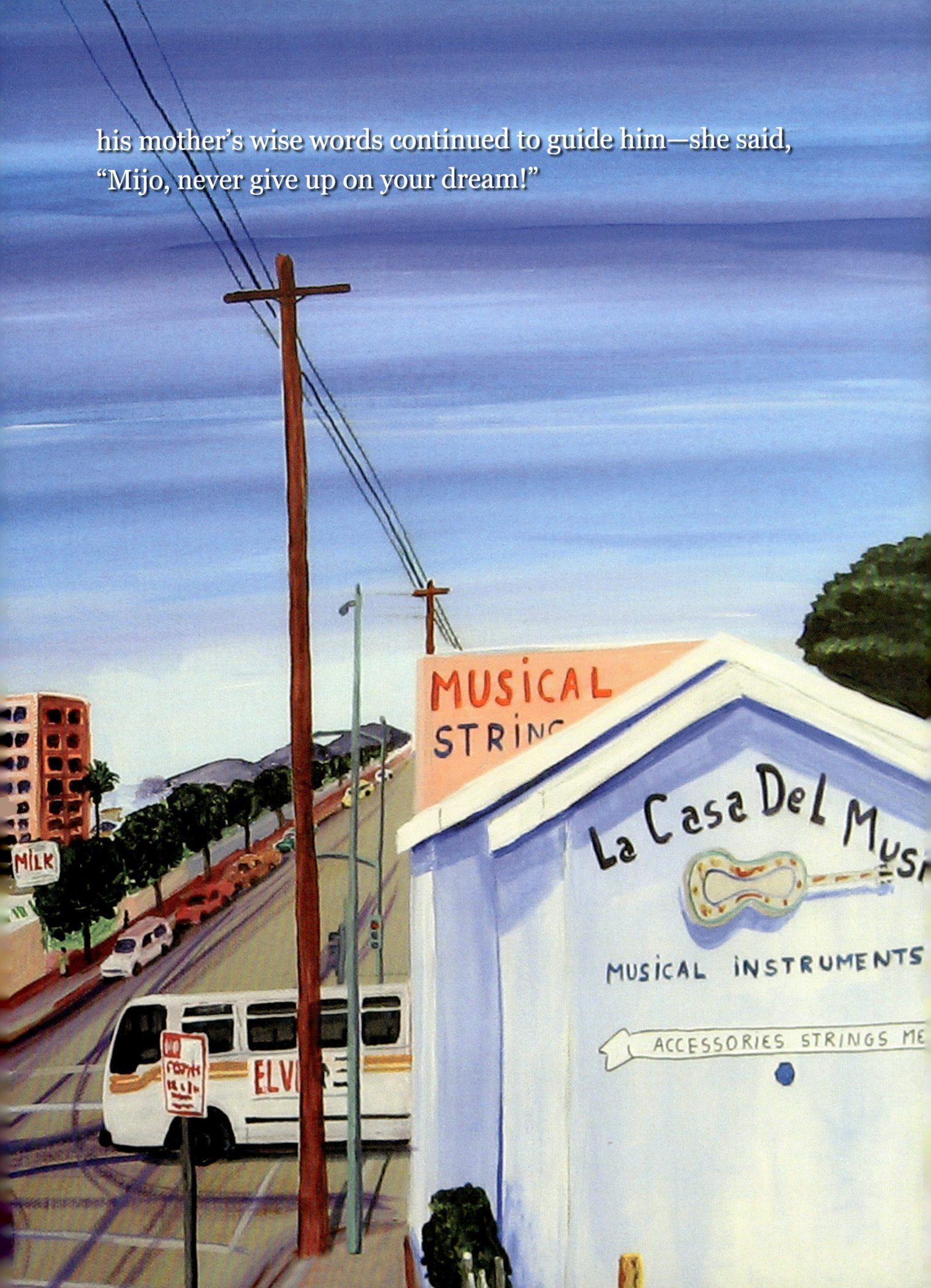

his mother's wise words continued to guide him—she said, "Mijo, never give up on your dream!"

Antonio once again ran for Mayor—and this time, he was elected! All of Los Angeles was proud, and his own community joyously welcomed Antonio Villaraigosa as the fourth Mexican-American Mayor of Los Angeles.

As Antonio gazed at Los Angeles from his City Hall window, he felt proud and humbled. A little boy who once shined shoes was now the Mayor of the City of Angels.

His dream had miraculously come true!

The City's new Mayor pledged to serve all Angelenos—and he took special pride in making his own Los Angeles barrio shine and sparkle, just like the shoes he shined so many years before. Antonio shined, shined, shined bright!

Antonio R. Villaraigosa is the 41st Mayor of Los Angeles. He was sworn in on July 1, 2005, and was elected to a second term in 2009. As President of the United States Conference of Mayors, he vigorously advocates for innovative public policy reforms to create jobs, improve public schools, and expand investment in America's transportation infrastructure.

As Mayor of Los Angeles, Villaraigosa fulfilled his pledge to make Los Angeles the safest big city in America, by building a 21st century transportation system, insisting on education reform, spurring economic development, and streamlining the City bureaucracy to ensure sustainability and green growth.

Prior to his tenure as Mayor, Villaraigosa served on the Los Angeles City Council and in the California State Assembly.

In 1994, Villaraigosa was elected to the California State Assembly, where he served as the first Assembly Speaker from Los Angeles in 25 years. During his tenure, Villaraigosa spearheaded efforts to modernize California schools, led a statewide initiative to provide parks and open space; funded an extensive water quality enforcement expansion, and authored the state health insurance program, Healthy Families.

Villaraigosa's civic activism began early—as a high school student, he worked for farm worker rights and led student walkouts to ensure social justice. After graduating from Theodore Roosevelt High School, he earned a Bachelor's Degree in History from UCLA, and also attended the People's College of Law.

As a union president, he represented civil rights workers and lawyers in six states. He also served as an organizer for the Service Employees International Union and United Teachers Los Angeles.

Born on January 23, 1953 in the Boyle Heights neighborhood of Los Angeles, Villaraigosa is the oldest of four children raised by a single mother, Natalia Delgado. He has four children, Marisela, Prisila, Antonio Jr. and Natalia, and two grandchildren.

Los Angeles Latino Mayors

Antonio Villaraigosa is the fourth Latino mayor of Los Angeles since California statehood in 1850. Elected in 2005, Villaraigosa is the first Latino to hold this office in 133 years. *Antonio Franco Coronel*, elected in 1853, was the first Latino mayor of Los Angeles. In 1856, *Manuel Requena* held office for 13 days after the former mayor resigned his position. *Cristobal Aguilar*, the last Latino mayor elected before Villaraigosa, served two terms from 1866 to 1870.

During his one year as mayor, Antonio Franco Coronel made great headway for the City by establishing the Department of Public Works. Today this department continues to provide services for our homes, neighborhoods, and businesses. He promoted civic improvements such as building a library, acknowledging historic landmarks, and even building an extension onto his house, which served as the first English-speaking theater in 1848.

Cristobal Aguilar served two separate terms as mayor. As a young man he witnessed the first municipal water system that pumped water from the Los Angeles River to the City center. Throughout his life Aguilar was involved in the politics of water. As Mayor, he vetoed the City Council vote to privatize the city waterworks in 1868. This decision helped set the stage for the establishment of the publically-owned Department of Water and Power years later. He soon realized that the most powerful position in Los Angeles was the head of the Los Angeles City Water Company, a post he assumed after his second term as mayor.

Los Angeles Latino Mayors historical recount prepared by the
Director of Education & Programs for LA Plaza de Cultura y Artes, *Cindi Dale*

LA Plaza Mission Statement

The mission of LA Plaza de Cultura y Artes is to celebrate and cultivate an appreciation for the enduring and evolving influence of Mexican and Mexican American culture, with a specific focus upon the unique Mexican American experience in Los Angeles and Southern California.

LA Plaza de Cultura y Artes is one of the nation's premier Mexican American cultural centers. Providing an experience unlike any other, LA Plaza's interactive exhibits and dynamic programs invite visitors to explore as well as contribute to the ongoing story of Mexican Americans in Los Angeles and beyond.

Located near the site where Los Angeles was founded in 1781, LA Plaza's 2.2-acre campus includes two historic and newly renovated buildings (the Vickrey-Brunswig Building and Plaza House) surrounded by 30,000 square feet of public garden. LA Plaza is a 501(c)(3) nonprofit organization, Federal Tax ID# 75-3059288. LA Plaza is an official project of Los Angeles County and a Smithsonian Affiliate.

501 North Main Street, Los Angeles, CA 90012
888-488-8083 • www.lapca.org